under
the bodhi tree

For Oliver – D.H.
For my dad – K.W.

Sounds True
Boulder, CO 80306

Published 2018

Book design by Lisa Kerans

Printed in China

Library of Congress Cataloging-in-Publication Data
Names: Hopkinson, Deborah, author. | Whitman, Kailey, illustrator.
Title: Under the Bodhi Tree : a story of the Buddha / by Deborah Hopkinson ;
    illustrated by Kailey Whitman.
Description: Boulder, CO : Sounds True, 2018. | Audience: Ages 4–8.
Identifiers: LCCN 2017056008 (print) | LCCN 2018002670 (ebook) |
    ISBN 9781683642497 (ebook) | ISBN 9781683641537 (hardcover)
Subjects: LCSH: Gautama Buddha]—Juvenile literature.
Classification: LCC BQ892 (ebook) | LCC BQ892 .H67 2018 (print) |
    DDC 294.3/63 [B]—dc23
LC record available at https://lccn.loc.gov/2017056008

10 9 8 7 6 5 4 3 2

Under the bodhi tree

a Story of the Buddha

Deborah Hopkinson

illustrations by Kailey Whitman

sounds true
BOULDER, COLORADO

In a long-ago time
and a faraway place,
a baby boy was born.

His name was Prince Siddhartha.

Before his birth,
his mother dreamed
of a beautiful white elephant.
The wise men said it was a sign
the baby would be special.

And he was.
Just like babies
then and now,
and everywhere.

And just like you.

The baby grew to be
a kind and gentle child.

Once, he found a wounded swan
and nursed it back to health
so it could soar
across the sky again.

The little prince wanted
to spread his wings, too.

But his father said,

"You must stay here,
away from the world,
where I can keep you safe
from any pain or sorrow."

And so Siddhartha grew up behind the garden walls
of a rich and splendid palace. He had new, fine clothes,
a grand white horse, the softest rice to eat.

But like children then and now, and everywhere, and just like you …

he longed to
discover the world.

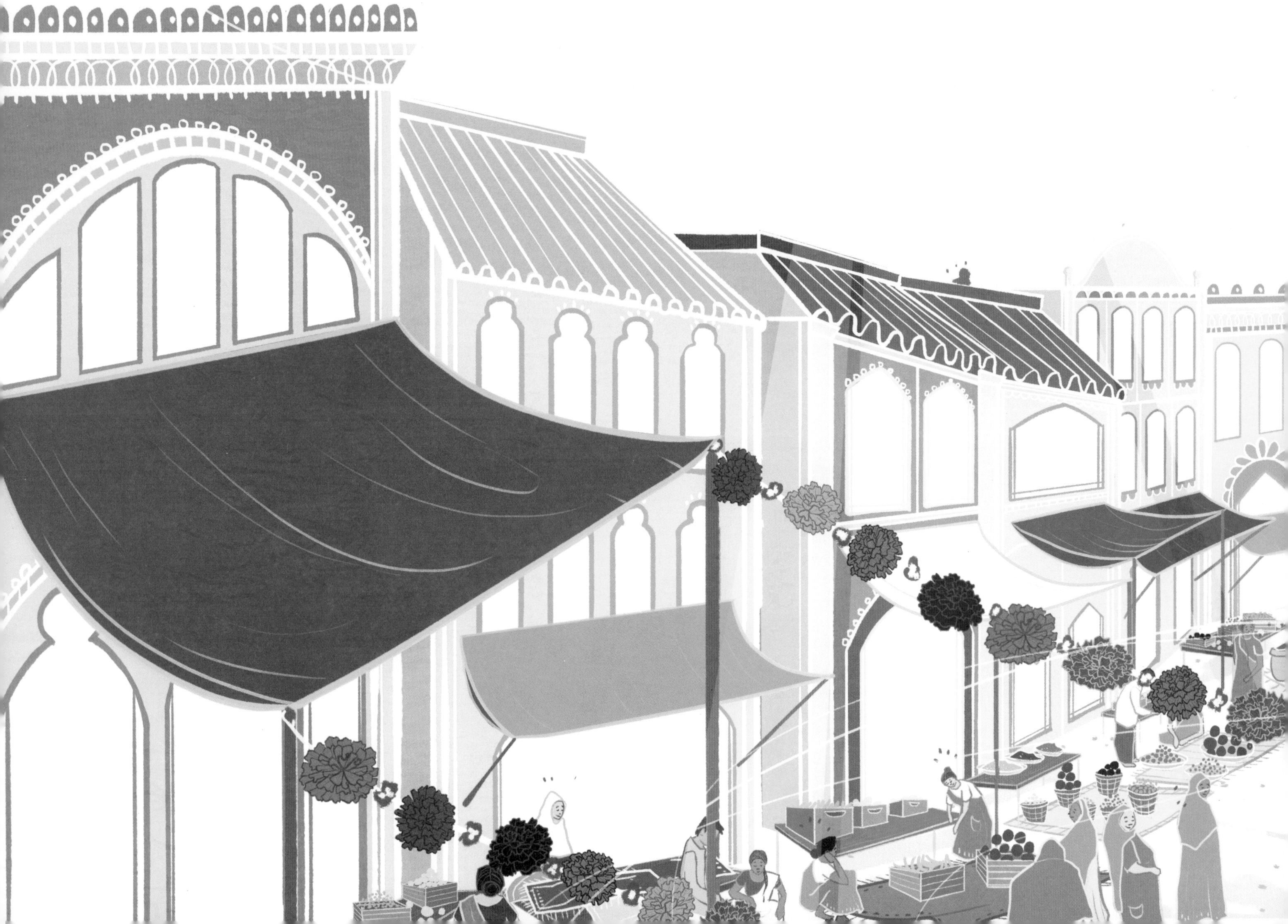

At last, when Siddhartha was a young man,
his father let him visit the great city.

The king ordered the mayor:
"Hold a festival in the market
with flowers, song, and dance.
My son must see only happy sights."

But, of course, the prince was curious
and wandered off to explore.
And that is how he first came to see
hardship, pain, and suffering.

First, he gave a sip of water
to a person lying sick with fever.

Next, he helped an old man
with an aching, crooked back
cross the road.

Then, he bowed his head
to share a grieving family's sorrow.

Siddhartha's heart felt heavy and his own eyes filled with tears. He could not stop wondering: *How can I help others?*

"You can do much good as a prince," the king told his troubled son. Siddhartha shook his head.

"Even the wisest ruler cannot stop sickness, old age, and death," he said. "I want to find a way to help people live in ease and peace."

And so, like seekers then and now,
and everywhere, the prince
set off to find his way,
just as you may
do someday.

At first, Siddhartha looked
to others for answers.
He journeyed far and long
and followed many different paths.

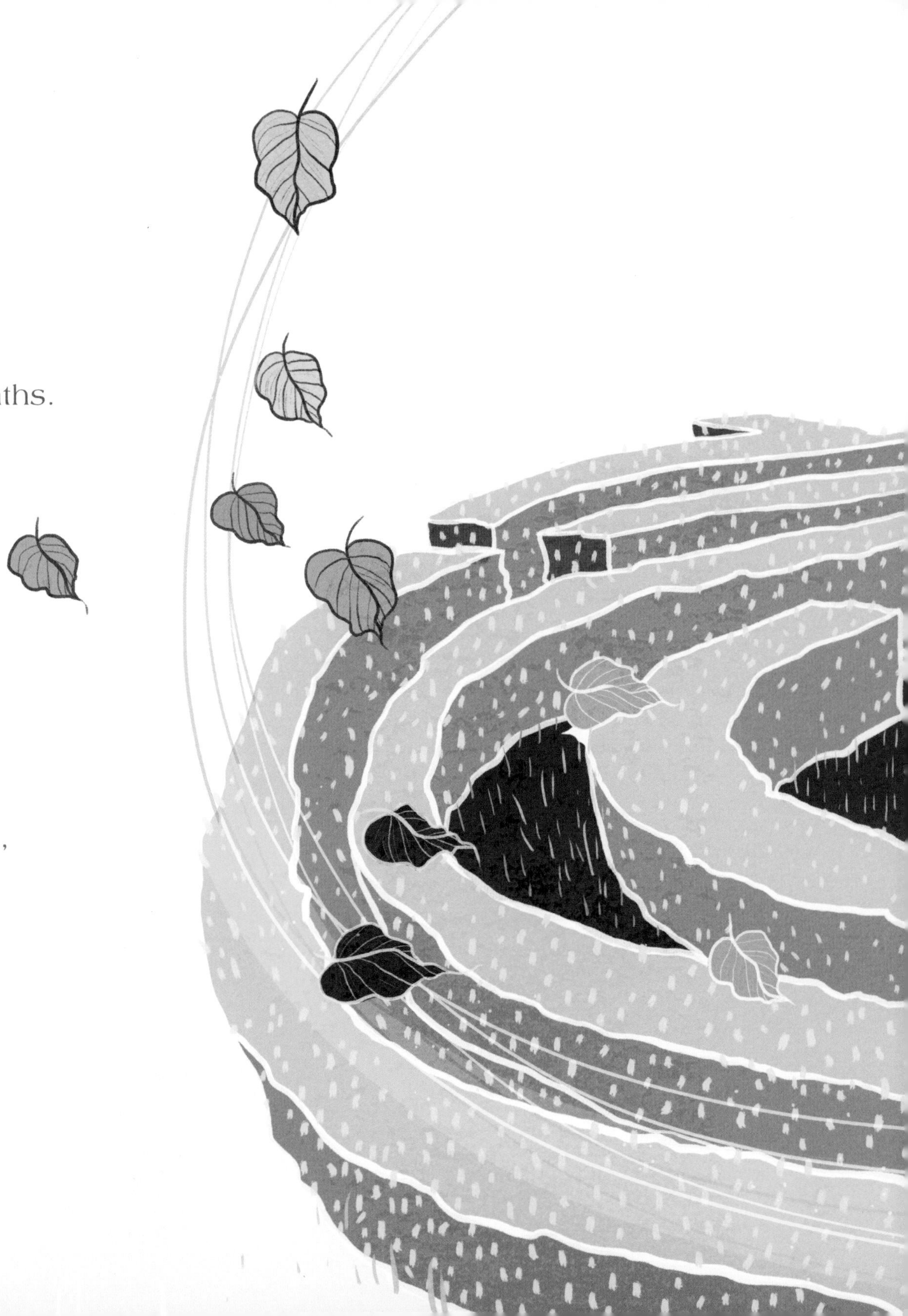

But he still felt lost,
like a little ship in a stormy sea,
tossed by wind and waves.

One day, Siddhartha
came upon the welcoming
shade of a tall, majestic tree.

His spirits rose and he thought,
Perhaps the answer is inside me.
I will stay in this pleasant grove
until I find a way to peace.
Then I can teach others, too.

And so Siddhartha crossed
his legs in quiet meditation.

Many days passed.
Raindrops fell.
Cool breezes blew.
The sun beat down.

And still Siddhartha sat,
sheltered by the rustling,
heart-shaped leaves
of the old and lovely tree.

Once, a woman named Sujata passed by
and thought, *He looks weak and hungry.*

She brought him sweetened milk and rice.
She smiled and said, "Please accept this gift.
If you are hungry, you should eat."

Siddhartha tipped back the bowl
to taste the delicious treat.
The rice and milk was warm and sweet!

"Thank you for your kindness," he said.

On that clear and brilliant night,
waves still rippled
the surface of his mind.
But now the prince just let
his fears and worries come and go
and kept on breathing mindfully,
in and out, deep and slow.

Soon, even the sighing,
heart-shaped leaves
grew still—
as serene as
Siddhartha's mind.

And then,
just before dawn,
he looked up.
In the eastern sky,
a bright planet appeared:
the morning star.

At that moment,
like the swan so long ago,
Siddhartha felt himself soar,
aware, free, and fully alive.
His worries fell away,
and he saw clearly
that all things fit together—
big and small,
hard and easy,
joyful and sad—

all part of one wondrous world.

In a time long ago
and a place far away,
a baby boy was born.
His name was Prince Siddhartha.

Today, we call him the Buddha,
the Awakened One.

Buddha did not stay alone
under the heart-shaped leaves
of the sacred Bodhi Tree.

Instead, he rose
and went into the world to
show the way of peace
to others...

then and now,
and everywhere.

And yes, of course,
to you and me.

About the Buddha

Siddhartha Gautama, the boy who grew up to be called the Buddha, was indeed a real person. But he lived so long ago we can't even be certain of the dates of his life and death. Scholars believe Siddhartha was born in Lumbini, which was part of northern India in ancient times but is now in Nepal. It's said that Queen Maya, wife of a king or clan chief named Śuddhodana, gave birth probably sometime around 623 BCE. Buddha's birth is usually celebrated on April 8.

His mother died soon after his birth, and Siddhartha was raised by his father and his mother's sister, Mahapajapati. Stories about his life include the incident with the wounded swan, as well as his first encounters with sickness, old age, and death. It's also said that his beautiful white horse, Kanthaka, died of a broken heart when Siddhartha left home on his spiritual quest. By then, he was married to a cousin named Yasodharā and had a son, Rāhula.

Siddhartha explored yoga and other spiritual paths, including fasting from food. It's said that when he came to an ancient fig tree in Bodh Gaya, he vowed not to rise before attaining enlightenment. Scriptures include the story of Sujata bringing him a special rice milk pudding.

Since Buddha's time, the tree (*Ficus religiosa*) has become known as a Bodhi Tree. It has beautiful, heart-shaped leaves known for their constant swaying. At Bodh Gaya, there is a tree that pilgrims visit which is believed to be a descendent of that ancient sacred tree.

Buddha's teachings are called the *dharma* and focus on mindfulness, nonviolence, and compassion. The *sangha* is the community, which includes people the world over. Many Buddhist traditions include mindful breathing and meditation, which anyone can learn to do.